SKETCH BOOK

For Keep's Sake
Add a Date!

_____

We hope everyone is having fun creating art in their Dibble Dabble Sketchbook!

Picturing the kids happily honing and building their skills while having fun with a book is what makes us *go* ~ at Dibble Dabble Press.

That *smile factor* is our reward and we strive to make sure that magic is in all the children's books we make.

Please stop by for a look at the other great fun and skill building Activity & Handwriting Practice books made special, just for the kids.

dibbledabblepress.com or *amazon.com/dibbledabblepress*

We would also be extra special grateful for your review ... on Amazon It really matters!

Thank You!

Made in the USA
Las Vegas, NV
19 December 2024